Math on the Job

Math at the Train Station

Tracey Steffora

Chicago, Illinois

Edited by Dan Nunn and Abby Colich
Designed by Victoria Allen
Picture research by Tracy Cummins
Production control by Vicki Fitzgerald

Printed and bound in China by Leo Paper Group

15 14 13 12
10 9 8 7 6 5 4 3 2 1

Library of Congress Cataloging-in-Publication Data
Steffora, Tracey.
  Math at the train station / Tracey Steffora.
     p. cm.—(Math on the job)
  Includes index.
  ISBN 978-1-4329-7154-0 (hb)—ISBN 978-1-4329-7161-8 (pb)
1. Railroad stations—Juvenile literature. 2. Mathematics—
Juvenile literature. I. Title.

TF148.S833 2013
513—dc23   2012013379

Acknowledgments
The author and publishers are grateful to the following for
permission to reproduce copyright material: Alamy:
pp. 5 (© Patrick Eden), 9 (© David Mark); Corbis:
p. 11 (© Construction Photography); Getty Images:
pp. 12 (AFP PHOTO PATRICK KOVARIK), 13 (Eric Hood);
Newscom: p. 6 (ZUMA Press); Photoshot: p. 7 (© Rafael
Ben-Ari/Chameleons Eye); Shutterstock: pp. 4 (John Leung),
8 (Ungor), 10 (auremar), 14 (Frances L Fruit), 16 (ARENA
Creative), 18 (joyfull), 19 (apiguide), 20 (Don Long),
21 (PaulPaladin), 22a (Ungor), 22b (ARENA Creative),
22c (apiguide); Superstock: p. 15 (© imagebroker.net).

Front cover photograph of a Tokyo train station reproduced
with permission from Alamy (© Picture Contact BV).

Back cover photograph a young man driving a tram
reproduced with permission from Shutterstock (auremar).

Every effort has been made to contact copyright holders
of any material reproduced in this book. Any omissions
will be rectified in subsequent printings if notice is given
to the publisher.

Contents

Math at the Train Station

People work at the train station.

People use math at the train station.

Counting

cashier

The cashier counts money.

conductor

The conductor counts tickets.

platform

The platforms have numbers.

How many platforms can
you count? (answer on page 22)

Measuring

engineer

The engineer drives the train.

The engineer measures how far.

how fast

The engineer measures how fast.

Which is faster? The person or the train? (answer on page 22)

Time

The conductor knows what time
a train leaves.

The conductor knows what time
a train arrives.

schedule

The schedule shows what time each train leaves.

Schedule	
City	**Departure Time**
Boston	7:30 a.m.
New York	8:00 a.m.
Newark	8:15 a.m.
Philadelphia	9:00 a.m.

What time does the train to New York leave? (answer on page 22)

Shapes

These workers build the tracks.

straight line

Some tracks are straight.

curved line

Some tracks are curved.

Are these tracks straight or curved?

(answer on page 22)

Answers

page 9: There are two platforms.

page 13: The train is faster.

page 17: The train leaves at 8:00 a.m. (a.m. means in the morning).

page 21: The tracks are curved.

Picture Glossary

 **platform** raised area where people get on and off trains

 **schedule** list that shows the time things happen

 **track** metal rails on which trains travel

Index

Notes for parents and teachers

Math is a way that we make sense of the world around us. For the young child, this includes recognizing similarities and differences, classifying objects, recognizing shapes and patterns, developing number sense, and using simple measurement skills.

Before reading
Connect with what children know.
Allow children to share any experience they have riding trains. Talk about the different jobs people have at the train station and on board trains.

After reading
Build upon children's curiosity and desire to explore.
If available, have a set of toy train tracks available in both straight and curved shapes. Discuss the difference between "straight" and "curved" and why straight tracks are used in real life (along a city street, pulling into a station, etc.) and curved tracks are sometimes needed (to go around a mountain, etc.). Have them sort the tracks into two piles. Extend by showing how curved tracks can make a circle and how inserting straight tracks changes this shape.

Reptile World
Alligators

by Vanessa Black

Bullfrog Books

Ideas for Parents and Teachers

Bullfrog Books let children practice reading informational text at the earliest reading levels. Repetition, familiar words, and photo labels support early readers.

Before Reading

- Discuss the cover photo. What does it tell them?

- Look at the picture glossary together. Read and discuss the words.

Read the Book

- "Walk" through the book and look at the photos. Let the child ask questions. Point out the photo labels.

- Read the book to the child, or have him or her read independently.

After Reading

- Prompt the child to think more. Ask: Have you ever seen an alligator? Where were you? What was it doing?

Bullfrog Books are published by Jump!
5357 Penn Avenue South
Minneapolis, MN 55419
www.jumplibrary.com

Library of Congress Cataloging-in-Publication Data

Names: Black, Vanessa, author.
Title: Alligators / by Vanessa Black.
Other titles: Bullfrog books. Reptile world.
Description: Minneapolis, MN: Jump!, Inc. [2017]
Series: Reptile world
Audience: Ages 5–8. | Audience: K to grade 3.
Includes bibliographical references and index.
Identifiers: LCCN 2015046705
ISBN 9781620313794 (hardcover: alk. paper)
Subjects: LCSH: Alligators—Juvenile literature.
Classification: LCC QL666.C925 B53 2017|
DDC 597.98/4—dc23
LC record available at http://lccn.loc.gov/2015046705

Editor: Jenny Fretland VanVoorst
Series Designer: Ellen Huber
Book Designer: Lindaanne Donohoe
Photo Researcher: Lindaanne Donohoe

Photo Credits: Alamy, 4, 5, 6–7, 14, 23br; Corbis, 8, 8–9, 23bl; iStock, 1, 15, 18–19, 20–21, 22, 23tr, 24; Shutterstock, cover, 3, 10; SuperStock, 11, 12–13, 16–17, 23tl.

Printed in the United States of America at Corporate Graphics in North Mankato, Minnesota.

Table of Contents

Later, Gator!

A gator digs.

She has long claws.

She gets reeds.

She gets grass.

nest

6

She makes a big pile.

What is it?

It is a nest!

She lays 16 eggs.
Now she will
guard the nest.

Oh, no!

Here comes a raccoon.

He wants the eggs.

Watch out!
Alligators have short legs.
But they move quickly.

11

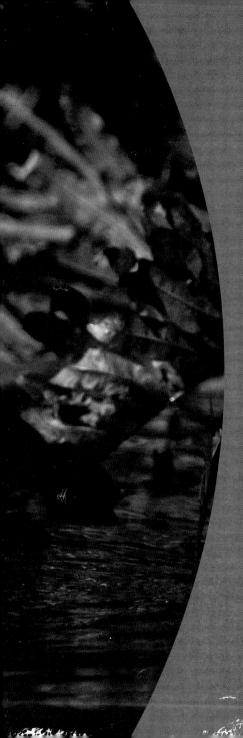

Chomp!
The mother grabs
with her sharp teeth.

Now she eats.

This gator ate a turtle.

He is full.

He basks in the sun.

It makes him warm.

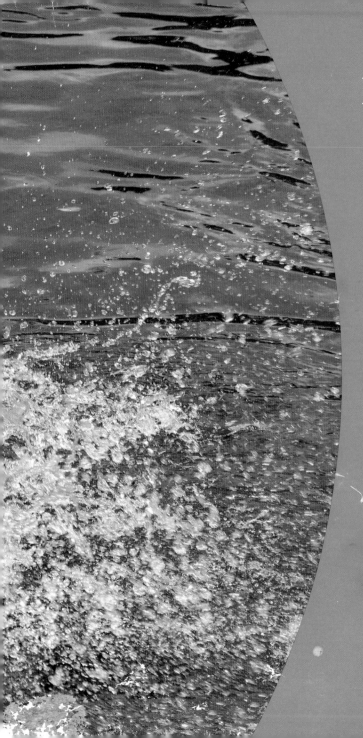

He will cool off
in the water.

Splash!

19

Gators are fast swimmers.

Their long tails
propel them.

See you later, alligator!

Parts of an Alligator

scutes
Alligators have hard, bony plates on their backs called scutes. They help protect their bodies.

snout
A part that sticks out from an alligator's body; an alligator's nose is at the end of its snout.

tail
Alligators have long, strong tails that help them swim fast.

jaws
Alligators have powerful jaws that can open very wide and snap shut quickly.

Picture Glossary

bask
To lay or sit in the sun to soak up the warm rays.

propel
To push forward.

guard
To keep watch, protect; to look out for danger.

reeds
Thin, tall grasses that grow in wet areas.

Index

To Learn More

Learning more is as easy as 1, 2, 3.

1) Go to www.factsurfer.com

2) Enter "alligators" into the search box.

3) Click the "Surf" button to see a list of websites.

With factsurfer.com, finding more information is just a click away.